Turkeys That Fly And Turkeys That Don't

By Allan Fowler

Consultants

Robert L. Hillerich, Professor Emeritus,
Bowling Green State University, Bowling Green, Ohio;
Consultant, Pinellas County Schools, Florida

Lynne Kepler, Educational Consultant

Fay Robinson, Child Development Specialist

CHILDRENS PRESS®
CHICAGO

Design by Beth Herman Design Associates
Photo Research by Feldman & Associates, Inc.

Library of Congress Cataloging-in-Publication Data

Fowler, Allan.
    Turkeys that fly and turkeys that don't / by Allan Fowler.
      p. cm. – (Rookie read-about science)
    ISBN 0-516-06029-5
    1. Turkeys–Juvenile literature. [1. Turkeys.]
  I. Title. II. Series.
QL696.G254F68   1994
598.6'19–dc20
                                94-14765
                                      CIP
                                        AC

Would you believe this
is a turkey?

No, it doesn't look too much like the bird people eat at Thanksgiving. Yet it is a turkey — a wild turkey.

Hundreds of years ago, the only turkeys were wild turkeys.

They lived in North America
and Central America.

America's
Indians used
turkey meat
for food.
They used
turkey feathers
to make
headdresses and
to decorate
their clothes.

Wild turkeys were eaten
by the Pilgrims at the first
Thanksgiving feast in 1621.

8

Many families still have turkey for dinner on Thanksgiving. Turkeys are often eaten at other holidays, too — or at any other time.

Some poultry farmers began
raising wild turkeys from
Mexico a long time ago.
They learned how to breed
bigger and meatier turkeys . . .

that looked like this.

Wild turkeys became
domestic turkeys — the
big birds we eat today.

Farmers in most parts of
the world now raise turkeys.

Wild turkeys still fly over
our country's forests.

But domestic turkeys can't fly.

Their shape is wrong
for flying, and they are
often too heavy to get
off the ground.

A full-grown male,
or tom, can weigh
as much as 50 pounds.

A full-grown female,
or hen, can weigh
more than 20 pounds.

Poultry farmers also grow
smaller breeds. Beltsville
Whites, like these, weigh
less than ten pounds.

Baby turkeys are called poults. They hatch from eggs about twice as big as chicken eggs.

Turkeys are sometimes called gobblers, after the "gobble, gobble" sound they make.

Many domestic turkeys
are white.

But other turkeys are colorful birds. Their heads and necks, where no feathers grow, are red and blue.

A fleshy wattle hangs from a turkey's throat . . . and there is a long, fleshy growth called a snood on its forehead. The snood hangs down over the bill.

24

A turkey with its tail
spread out like a fan
is very handsome.

This Bronze tom has
plumage, or feathers,
of a bronze or copper
color mixed with green.

You can tell it's a tom by
its size — and by the way
his feathers gleam like
metal in the sunlight.

If a small family bought a big Bronze, they would be eating turkey — or turkey hash — for days and days.

It's better if you don't have too much of a good thing —

even something as
tasty as turkey!

Words You Know

wild turkey

domestic turkey

Bronze

Beltsville Whites

poults

snood   wattle

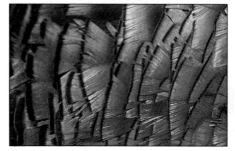

headdress   plumage

Index

About the Author

Allan Fowler is a free-lance writer with a background in advertising. Born in New York, he lives in Chicago now and enjoys traveling.

Photo Credits

©Reinhard Brucker – 6, 31 (left)

Grant Heilman Photography, Inc. – ©Grant Heilman, 17, 30 (bottom right); ©Jim Strawser, 18, 31 (top right)

©Bill Ivy – 27, 30 (bottom left)

PhotoEdit – ©Tony Freeman, 8; ©Jeff Greenberg, 10

Tom Stack & Associates – ©Joe McDonald, 19; ©Mike Bacon, 21; ©Wendy Shattil/Bob Rozinski, 24

SuperStock International, Inc. – 7; ©John Warden, Cover; ©Ron Dahlquist, 12; ©Leonard Lee Rue, 13; ©Rivera Collection, 29

Valan – ©John Fowler, 11, 15, 30 (top right); ©Pam Hickman, 20

VIREO – ©R. & N. Bowers, 3, 30 (top left)

Visuals Unlimited – ©John Bohlden, 5; ©Joe McDonald, 23, 31 (center right); ©Bill Banaszewski, 27 (inset), 31 (bottom right)

COVER: Turkey